YOUR KNOWLEDGE HAS VALUE

Bibliographic information published by the German National Library:

The German National Library lists this publication in the National Bibliography; detailed bibliographic data are available on the Internet at http://dnb.dnb.de .

Imprint:

Copyright © 2018 GRIN Verlag
Print and binding: Books on Demand GmbH, Norderstedt Germany
ISBN: 9783346054586

This book at GRIN:

https://www.grin.com/document/504948

Moniruzzaman Kiron

Advantages and Weaknesses of the Volkswagen Group (VW). Value Chain and SWOT Analysis

GRIN Verlag

GRIN - Your knowledge has value

Since its foundation in 1998, GRIN has specialized in publishing academic texts by students, college teachers and other academics as e-book and printed book. The website www.grin.com is an ideal platform for presenting term papers, final papers, scientific essays, dissertations and specialist books.

Visit us on the internet:

http://www.grin.com/

http://www.facebook.com/grincom

http://www.twitter.com/grin_com

Content

1.0 Company Background

Volkswagen Group (VW) is an automotive company founded in 1937. The automobile firm was founded by German Labour Front at Berlin, the capital of Germany. The current headquarters are located in Wolfsburg, Germany. VW has 120 production plants in 31countries. In manufacturing there are 626,715 workers who contribute to produce cars or to maintain ongoing relationships with customers, suppliers and partners in 153 countries. VW also has the Volkswagen brand, which is the focus of the Institute in the development of employee skills and language learning. Volkswagen Bank is a financial institution focused on savings and investment. Volkswagen is currently the largest automobile manufacturer in the world. (Beckwith, 2016)

Volkswagen's vision is to be recognized as a company that is defined in Market, and became the leader in sales and distribution of spare parts, reach economic services of excellence; development and growth are always characterized firm. The Group mission to offer vehicles that are attractive, safe and environmentally friendly can compete in an increasingly tough market and which set world standards in their each class (Volkswagenag.com). For the Volkswagen Group, **sustainability** means that businesses are conducted in a responsible and long-term basis. The company looks in benefit from the growth, customers and investors, society and of course benefiting employees. In this way, a good job and a careful treatment of resources and the environment form the basis for generating sustainable value. Next will be **responsibility for society**, Volkswagen supports projects that promote culture and the arts, education, science, health and sports. A company with global operations, VW has the responsibility of being responsible for the global society we cannot be met simply by applying for charity. Instead, Volkswagen took the individual and above all long-term commitment. For the Volkswagen Group, **corporate social responsibility (CSR)** has been a long time coming to a meaningful commitment to the local which is outside the factory gates. And promote social projects, cultural and social, Volkswagen sees themselves as a source of encouragement for the development of local economy and equal opportunities. VW support 200 projects around the world that are designed to improve the economic and social structure, placing emphasis on continuity and sustainability. Dr Herbert Diess is the Chairman of the company.

Since 2002, Volkswagen has been involved in one of the largest CSR initiative and the most important in the world. Forming the core values of the Global Compact, together with 12,000 companies from over 170 countries, the Volkswagen works in international CSR projects that range towards making the global economy more sustainable and more equitable.. With the reorientation of the Group, Volkswagen will be different, better company. But this process will take some time. Against this background Volkswagen allow members of the UN Global Compact during that time. According to the latest accounting report, Volkswagen have brought in losses with an amount of 1.86 million euros.

2.0 Environmental Analysis

2.1 Value Chain Analysis

2.1.1 Primary Activities

1. Inbound Logistics

   Volkswagen has 120 production plants across 31 countries. In 2016 about 75 million metric cubes of production materials were supplied globally for automobile production. Inbound logistics for Volkswagen comprises of two types. The first is the transportation of suppliers to the manufacturing plants in Germany; the second is the global inbound logistics which is transportation of supplies to the manufacturing plants all over the world. Volkswagen adds value to the inbound logistics as they ensure that the raw materials are supplied with precision as most of the materials are supplied within the European Production Network. Volkswagen group have a chain of around 8,500 suppliers. (Cavendish, 2002)

2. Operations

   Volkswagen Group offers passenger vehicles by the brands named Volkswagen and other subsidiaries such as Seat, Porsche, Bugatti, Audi, Bentley, Lamborghini and Skoda. They also sell commercial vehicles under Volkswagen Commercial Vehicles, Man and Scania.

The Group also sells motor vehicles under the brand, Ducati. The company sells 10.3 million vehicles in 2016.

Volkswagen offers automobile designing facilities under Italdesign Giuguiaro located in Moncailieri, Italy. Volkswagen also holds financing solutions as they provide financing, insurance and leasing to the customers. Named Volkswagen Financial Service, the sector has made an operating income of 1641 million Euros in 2016. (Volkswagen AG, 2010)

3. Outbound Logistics

Volkswagen supplies Passenger cars, Commercial Vehicles and Motor Vehicles in 153 countries. Volkswagen has distributed vehicles to the respective dealers through road, sea and air ways. Volkswagen has shipped 5.2 million vehicles to the destinations all over the world. Volkswagen has taken more efforts on distributing through sea as they have shipped around 2.5 million vehicles in more than 8700 shipments.

4. Marketing and Sales

Normally Volkswagen communicates and promotes the brand substantially through print and media advertising. The marketing methods of Volkswagen emphasize innovativeness and efficiency of the brand. Volkswagen sales activities are mainly focused on providing consistent satisfaction to the customers. The German manufacturer is currently focusing on new customer approaches. Volkswagen marketing strategy does not only provide satisfaction by delivering quality but also satisfying emotional demands as well. (Schultz, 2017)

5. Service

Volkswagen is known for its remarkable quality of service before and after the sale, which are one of their main sources of the firm's competitive advantage. The company looks to retain the highest satisfaction level of the customers by equipping precise feedback and resolution to the customer necessities. The company's service fixes vehicles according to the quality standards by providing the right people with the right tools.

2.1.2 Secondary Activities

1. Firm Infrastructure

   Volkswagen currently has buildings, property, factory plants and manufacturing plants with a worth of 54,033 million Euros. They have 120 production plants all over the world. The German automobile maker has formed with the Chinese automakers, FAW Group and SAIC Motors as a fixed term venture. Volkswagen has around 626,715 employees in 2016. Volkswagen has car themed buildings which have a height of 160 feet. These towers are made of silo-like glass and made to store cars. Volkswagen also have two museums in the headquarters Wolfsburg, Germany. The museum displays the history of the Volkswagen brand since its formation. The museum which is called AutoMuseum Volkswagen, lines up with vintage and classic cars the firm have produced (Graham, 2015).

2. Human Resource

   Volkswagen and the other subsidiaries have created their unique tailor-made training and development activities. Dual vocation training practices are one of the main activities of the firm's human resource. In 2016, Volkswagen recruited around 19,500 trainees involved in 60 dual vacation and apprentice schemes.

   The German firm structure holds a high value on job of the employees and their family members. The company's family-friendly human resource policies are one of the main reasons that led Volkswagen become on e of the world's distinguished employers. As a proportion of voluntary commitment, the company comes up with objective to increase the amount of recruiting women in European countries for a longer period. (King, 2017)

3. Technology Development

   Volkswagen is looking to find solutions for the future challenges. Volkswagen has brought technology development ranging from powerful engines to comfortable travelling. Volkswagen has brought up infotainment systems which provide more convenience with applications and navigation systems. Volkswagen has introduced car assistance systems such as blind spot sensor and emergency braking to reduce the

4

chances of car getting damaged. Volkswagen have brought up efficient engines such that produces for maximum power within the minimum consumption of the fuel. (Chicago Tribune, 2016)

4. Procurement

The company is trying harder to create an effective and efficient procurement organization. Volkswagen aims to build on abilities and strengths together with their suppliers. Volkswagen's primary aim is to become the finest competitive high performing procurement firm.

The company's procurement involves purchasing of production materials, services and capital expenditure centrally. The volume procured last year was about 149.1 billion Euros. The company and its subsidiaries are looking to develop the procurement strategy with uniform and digital processes. Volkswagen aims to connect a digitalized network, called Supplier Interaction Management to connect all the suppliers of the firm within the next five years. (Volkswagen Annual Report, 2015)

2.2 Porter's five forces

Threat of New Entrants:

A new firm in automobile industry requires a high amount of capital to compete with the existing firms. Along with the big capital, the new entrants would also require setting up network with regional dealers, obtain licensing and establish brand trust among the customers. Some of the competitors join hands with the current competitors as subsidiaries. Eventually the bigger firms in the industry reduce the threat of new entrants. So the threat of new entrants for Volkswagen is low. (Dediu, 2015)

Bargaining Power of Suppliers:

The demands of suppliers are low in automotive industry as they similar in supplying products in contrast with the quality and pricing. The switching are less as it is not difficult to change suppliers and therefore can reduce their power. There is a big amount of suppliers in the industry which gives the firm options to obtain even if one of their suppliers does not meet their standards. As these suppliers are reliant on the automobile manufacturers, the bargaining power of suppliers is low. (Uzwyshyn., 2013)

Bargaining Power of Buyers:

The automobile industry involves a huge number of companies which lead to reduce the switching costs. This leads to increase the bargaining power of buyers. However the identification of brand can give advantages over the rival firms. The consumer will stay loyal to the brand if they provide great satisfaction which can lead to decrease the bargaining power of buyers. In overall the bargaining power of buyers is high because the buyers have multiple options for the buyers to choose in purchasing a car.

Threat of Substitutes:

In cities and towns, people can travel through trains busses and cabs as they are easy to access and affordable. Along with this, the rising of fuel prices stimulate people to substitute which leads to increase the threat. However, owning a car is a requirement in this generation. Vehicles are considered as a commodity as most of the families at least hold one car. As cars are more affordable than ever it leads in reduce the threat. In overall, the threat of substitutes is medium. (Graham R. M., 2010)

Intensity of Rivalry:

There has been a significant growth in automobile industry in terms of quality and innovation. It is said that the automobiles are turning up to be more of a commodity than being luxury. It creates more opportunities as the demand increases. So the growth rate has an impact on the rivalry intensity. Since the fixed cost in the automobile industry is high, it causes rivalry because it is necessary to achieve more sales to make profit. Besides that, there is no much differentiation of products in the current automobile industry. The low differentiation of product causes an increase in rivalry. Also, the costs of switching are low for consumers. If a brand does not fulfill a customer's expectation, it is not hard to choose any other automobile brand, so that would cause an increase rivalry. In a nutshell, the intensity of rivalry is high in the world of automotive.

2.3 SWOT Analysis

Strength:

1. Operations well managed: One of the main strengths of the German automaker is, their operations are of high standards with an effective and efficient management. The Volkswagen Group consists of 12 subsidiaries where they can target different segment of customers. Their efforts have made the ranked seventh largest company in the world according to Fortune Global 100.

2. Research and Development: The vehicles of Volkswagen are well known in advanced technology. The company has invested further in research and development to bring diversifications in vehicles. Their effective efforts in R&D brought up technology development such as infotainment systems, car assistance systems and fuel efficient car and motor engines which provides great performance.

3. High Branding: Volkswagen is a demanded car automaker which produces vehicles of 28,000 quantities in a single day. The brands have a great market share in European markets and it extending all over the world. Their marketing strategy and advertising

have brought brand attraction to the customers. The after sales services have sustained their customers bringing brand loyalty, makes on the reasons why they are the largest automaker in the world.

4. Excellent Production Capabilities: Another strength of Volkswagen is of great production capabilities. The company extended production facility comprises of 120 production plants in 31 countries across the world. They have produced 10.3 million vehicles in 2016 which have made them the world's largest automaker in the world. They have extended the production by merging with Chinese automakers as they produce over 3.5 millions units' different models of Volkswagen and its other brands.

Weakness:

1. Controversy of the emission scandal: There was a scandal regarding the emission created by the Volkswagen vehicles which were above the Environmental Protection Standards. Due to this issue, around five million cars produced from 2009 till 2015 were recalled. This has affected the reputation of the company and stock prices fall down. The issue has brought the company losses of around 16.2 billion Euros.

2. Low market share: The brand positioning of Volkswagen is weak in some of the countries. In countries like the United States and India, the local and other multinational firms have take control of the market share. These companies have a significant sales figure making Volkswagen difficult to compete in the market For instance, USA is the second largest automobile market in the world and Volkswagen only owns 5% of the market share.

3. Parent brand not strengthened: Volkswagen Group invests a lot for advertising and other marketing strategies to the Volkswagen subsidiaries. But compared to the marquee brand less amount of money is invested. The company must look in investing to create more brand equity for the parent brand. The company has superior car models like Touareg and

Beetle which are a hit under the Volkswagen brand. But the brand does not create much marketing efforts, which is a necessity in the market.

4. High Cost Structure: Volkswagen produces the vehicles with efficiency and high quality. These cars are well equipped with advanced technological systems. When the company aims to provide vehicles in order to satisfy customers needs, the production costs of the car is also increasing. The high cost structure leads to increase the price of the vehicle which makes it unaffordable for the customers to purchase the vehicle.

Opportunities:

1. High Entry Barrier: One of the opportunities Volkswagen has is the high barriers for the new entrants in the automobile industry. A new automobile firm would require huge capital investment, establishment of production plants, obtain licensing, connections with suppliers and dealers and establish brand trust with the customers. The helps Volkswagen having less new rivals in the automobile industry.

2. Purchasing power is increasing: One of the opportunities Volkswagen have is the increase of purchasing power Vehicles are considered an luxury item before but in this generation, it is considered as a necessity as at least each family now owns a vehicle. Purchasing cars have much been much easier as different financing solutions like loans and installments have been provided by automobile companies. With the help of assistance from Volkswagen Financial Service, the sales of Volkswagen vehicles have increased rapidly.

3. Manufacturing Fuel Efficient: Fuel efficient ars like Electric cars and Hybrid cars are now the future of the automobile industry and Volkswagen should take initiatives on it. Car manufacturers like Toyota and Tesla have started producing fuel efficient cars, Volkswagen's strong research and development can be a major factor in bringing these vehicles to the market. In the future, if fuel becomes expensive and governments will

look towards renewable sources for energy, these fuel efficient cars can be a hit in the automobile industry.

4. High Potential Market: Volkswagen must look into the emerging countries. The demand of the cars increases along with the growing GDP of the particular country. As the expansion of Volkswagen cars is broadening, it can help in gain more market share in these countries. Volkswagen also must scout to localize the vehicles and target the customers according to the local requirement standards.

Threats:

1. Strong Competition: The Company is facing with an intense rivalry with the leading automobile manufacturers and the new companies in the markets. In the Chinese and Indian markets, the local competitors are competing by offering lower prices to the vehicles which quality might be built similar. Companies like Toyota and Tesla are well known in the its electric and hybrid cars segment making it difficult for Volkswagen to compete. These factors have made the company's production capacity farther than the demand as 31 million units of vehicles were overproduced in 2015.

2. Changing Customer Choices: One of the threats Volkswagen face is different choices is available for the customers which can cause in shifting the demand of the customers. The emission scandal has brought a negative impression to the customers. Most of the cars were recalled due to the engine defect on the models. This could lead customers' options to purchase vehicles from other competitors or choose substitutes.

3. Fluctuating Fuel Prices: Non-renewable resources like Petrol and diesel are been in higher demand than ever before leading to increasing the prices of the fuels used in cars. Even though hybrid and electric cars are introduced. Most of the cars are used by these

demanded fuels. This factor can change people to travel through public transportation affecting the demand of Volkswagen vehicles.

4. Different regulations in different countries: The governments in each countries aims to protect and assist the local car manufacturers over the multinational car automakers. These governments will establish policies which will support the local automakers. They propose high product taxes on the multinational automakers and government will keep the profits for the country. These factor will bring threat to a multinational company like Volkswagen.

3.0 Strategic Competitive Advantage and Major Weaknesses

The first competitive strategic advantage of Volkswagen is:

Operations are well managed: The Company is huge as far as operations. Taking care of a creation of near 27000 cars a day alongside co-ordinations, production network and different operations is difficult. Thus, one might say that the operations management of Volkswagen is fabulous. Accenture is the consultancy partner of Volkswagen and handles all its product and equipment requirements. Other than Accenture, Volkswagen has a wide range of different partners for accounting, inventory network and others.

The second competitive strategic advantage of Volkswagen:

Research and development: Volkswagen cars are known to have high innovation inbuilt and are trusted for their performance. Volkswagen has as of late wandered into Hybrid cars and motorcycles are being included the portfolio as well. Other than this, the R&D of all sub brands gives items past desires as it has been always developing new creative designs and advanced features are been included from model to model. This can ultimately help people gain more attention for having more choices.

The first major weakness of Volkswagen is:

Controversy and fraud about the emission of the cars caused global brand loss:

Volkswagen has been cheating in emission tests by making its cars show up far less polluting than they are. This has been proved by the U.S environmental assurance agency by finding that 482,000 Volkswagen diesel cars on American streets were known to be emitting up to 40 times more harmful toxic fumes than allowed and Volkswagen has since conceded the cheat influences 11 million cars around the world.

It is continued by low market share in the U.S automotive market:
The stats shows Volkswagen share of the U.S market has decreased the sales from 3% to 2%, this shows that there are a lot of competitors in the U.S that has caused them to low market share.

4.0 Recommendations

4.1 Strategic Recommendations

Strength

1. **Operations well managed**

Volkswagen is huge and well known automotive company all around the world. Volkswagen Company is huge in terms of operation. In Germany, there are few towns that are literally dependent on the company for employment. The production handled by the company is close to 27000 cars per day including with their supply chain, logistic and other operations included. The world knows that the company's management is excellent but we don't know how difficult and challenging it is to handle and sustain their operations. To sustain their operations as the company grows and face different types of challenges along the way, Volkswagen will have to focus on their marketing and sales to keep their operations running smoothly.

Besides that with good marketing the company will not only be able to sustain their operations but in fact they will be able to attract new customers in different segments of their operations by promoting their specific products to their targeted customers. With good marketing skills applied to their operating system, the company will be able to expand their business into new market segments even though the company is well known but there are still few countries where Volkswagen position remains weak, for example India and Pakistan. The company should study and understand the targeted market before making a move, by applying their marketing skills afterwards will help them to increase their sales which will make the company to grow even more and will be able to achieve their goals by maximizing their profit. The company will have to practice different marketing strategy to achieve those goals.

At the same time, the company will have to improve their services in the process of expanding and maintaining their operations worldwide. Volkswagen is well known for their remarkable services, but they need to try things differently to achieve something new in other countries. At first the management will try to understand the culture and the income inequality in that country to provide the services that will suit their needs and taste. To provide these services the management should provide special services to their employees that operate in different market segments. This will help the company to deliver the services that suits the people in that market. This will help the company to gain more customers and even create even more loyal customers.

To make these strategies successful, the company will have to take risk and explore other countries and use their resources and invest on their employees so that the training provided to them will help them to operate well in the new segments that they discovered.

2. Research and development

Volkswagen cars are known to have high innovation inbuilt and are trusted for their performance. Recently Volkswagen had wandered into Hybrid autos and bikes are being included in the portfolio. Other than this, the R&D of all sub brands gives their products beyond expectation.

The company has a very strong brand image and high innovation in their research and development are well known around the world, even with this good record the company still has so much to work on their technology development because the company has so much to improve to compete with the most leading innovative companies in the world. Even though the company had delivered satisfaction to their customers, but as the time passes and the technology grows,

13

the customers will demand for new products. To make this happen the company will have to invest and use their resources to come up with new models of vehicles to compete with their fierce competitors that are taking research and development very seriously.

The company should work hard on their research and development and follow the latest trend such as coming up with resources and come up with the technology that can help them to create driverless cars which had been demanded by many. Google Company had invested their resources to come up with that car and are currently gaining profit and controlling that market.

Volkswagen will have to take the risk to invest on this new idea and will cost them a lot but it is important for the company to get this technology to gain more market share and deliver the satisfaction to certain customers in different segments. Because for a huge company like Volkswagen, should aim to come up with new innovative products that will satisfy the needs and wants of their customer.

Technological innovations like these will not only the customers exited but it will also profit the company which will fund them to grow even more and install the latest technologies in their products. The risk taken will benefit the company as the company already has a very strong brand image. Even though the company has good department or team that handle the research and development, with these upgrades the company will be able to improve that sector of the company by using the latest technologies and dominate the market that they choose to operate in.

It can be said that that the risk taken by the company to implement these technologies will benefit them in different manners. With their existing skills it is believed that these new creation can be very successful and will help the company to compete better with their competitors in the market and control most of the market shares.

Weakness

1. Controversy and fraud about the emission

A huge time scandal breaks through the media and had spread around the market the company operates which negatively affected the strong brand image that the company has. Near 5 million cars were come back to the company and the company had lost more than 15 million – a move which dependably harms the top brand. Trust was broken particularly on the grounds that this choice of introducing the wrong programming originated from the top administration of the organization.

This issue had seriously affected the brand image that the company had worked so hard to create. This issue not only had made people question about the problem on the emission but it had also raised various types of questions among the consumers which made them wonder what else could the company are hiding. The top level management was directly involved in this huge scandal. This had put the company in the risk when their shares started to falling when the almost 5 million of their cars were returned to them. This problem did not only concern the brand users but also other people due to the radiation and gas caused by their products. The competitors took this opportunity to win over the market shares. Competitors labeled Volkswagen as cheaters and fraud as they had cheated the emission by using the 'defeat device' tested back in 2015.

Even though, the managers had took responsibility and claimed that 'screwed up' and had took back all the faulty cars. This does not totally repair their brand image which had been damaged by the emission scandal. To gain back their strong brand image, the words of their managers won't make much different but the actions of the company will, the people responsible handling those involved in the scandal should terminate those staff and replace them with new line of managers that are more responsible and can manage the company and its decisions the right way. This action will gain the confidence and trust of their customers. To show to the customer that the company is really trying to fix their mistake, that should come up with a different technology advancement that give them the ability to create advanced green cars.

The new managers will have to adapt to a new technology which are emission free and use a much more proper and safer way in handling their products. A new system must be applied to safe the company's sale from keep falling.

The company will face a huge risk managing this and will cost them a lot to come up with environmental-friendly but with their reserves and asset it will make things as it was.

2. Low market share in the US automotive market.

The performance of the company in the US is poor due to the intensive rivalry among the competitors in the state. Volkswagen controls a little percentage of the market share in the US. Back in 2015 the company only controlled 4.5% of the market shares, this is because they had been facing some car manufacturers in the market which have a very strong brand image in US. Some experts' believe that the company should exit the market after the scandal occurred. Few of the huge competitors the company face is General motors, ford, Toyota and more.

To gain the market shares, the company will have to try things differently and study the market more detail before operating in that specific market. The main reason that their products didn't not gain much attentions is due to the high prices for their cars. The economy in the US is not balanced which blocks the consumers to spend more money on these cars.

Volkswagen will have to invest more and come up with products which are much cheaper with good performance overall to satisfy the needs and wants of the consumers in US. Besides that, the company should come up with unique designs and features due to the threat of substitutes and a large number of competitors. To gain the consumers attention in that market, the can come up with large SUVs that suits their taste and preferences. To make their products well known, the company should improve their marketing skills.The company should use their resources and asset gained from other market where they own a good amount of market shares and invest it in the US so they can start dominating the market.

4.2 Justification of Strategy

For sustaining the competitive advantages and overcoming the major weaknesses, the company must look to invest a high amount of capital. In 2016, Volkswagen currently has 30.14 billion Euros. For sustaining the effective management the company should focus on bringing employee training schemes which should be budgeted at least 8 million Euros. This scheme would take a period 4 years to sustain the management.

The company should to build more research and development facilities in different geographical locations for further technological advancements. The company should budget around 750 million Euros and would take approximately 5 years to build the facilities.

The company should look up to bring marketing strategies like more customer benefits such as reducing the price of the car for a limited period. The scheme is to give customer allowance which will help to increase the brand loyalty and forget the emission scandal. This should be implemented in the famous models which are Touareg and Beetle. The company should budget around half a billion Euros and will take approximately four years.

In order to increase the market share, the country look to merge with the local companies, for further production and capturing the automobile market of that particular country. The acquisition plan will not be pended the company have to make sure that it must benefit both Volkswagen and the particular local company. The period would tale around three years with effective marketing and advertising efforts, which Volkswagen should budget around 350 million euros.

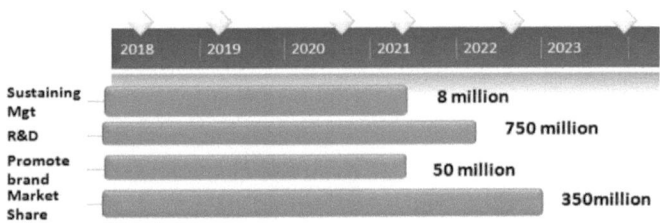

Figure 1: Budget Forecast.

5.0 Conclusion

For a huge company like Volkswagen it takes a lot of effort to maintain their great brand reputation, to sustain that they have to make sure they fulfill the needs and wants of their customers and satisfy them. Although the brand portfolio includes brands like Skoda, Bugatti and Lamborghini the company still ranks high in the mind of customers. Even so having some problems in the automotive industry recently they must start looking forward and try finding solution as it might affect their brand image which can cause them huge loss and maintain the trust and build a relation among their customers as well. Volkswagen items are strongly connected with so much feelings as security and sense of pride. Quality and upper-mid cost focusing on essentially add to those emotions. However, Volkswagen tends to build its marketing efforts around specialized components of vehicles. Indeed, even the motto of organization states so: Das Auto — The Car. Thus, Volkswagen focuses on those customers that acknowledge generally innovation, accuracy and quality. Volkswagen is capable of expanding their business to a next level where they can gain most of the market shares in the automotive industry.

References

Beckwith, J. (2016). Volkswagen is world's largest car maker over first half of 2016.

Cavendish, M. (2002). Encyclopedia of World Geography. Andromedia Oxford Ltd.

Chicago Tribune. (2016). Volkswagen bets on new technology to bounce back from crisis.

Dediu, H. (2015). The Entrant's Guide to The Automobile Industry.

Graham, P. (2015). The Building Sector's continuous 'Volkswagen' Moment.

Graham, R. M. (2010). Drive No More: 6 Alternatives to Your Car. *Treehugger* .

King, J. (2017). VW HR head says cultural reform will 'take a bit of time'. *Left Lane* .

Richard, M. G. (n.d.). Drive No More: 6 Alternatives to Your Car. *Treehugger* , 201o.

Schultz, E. (2017). Thinking New: Inside Volkswagen's Plans to Become Relevant Again. *Advertising Age* .

Uzwyshyn., R. (2013). The US Auto Industry in 2013: Five Forces to Consider . *Automotive Indutries Online* .

Volkswagen AG. (2010). *Volkswagen Aktiengesellschaft Annual Report 2009.*

Volkswagenag.com. (n.d.). Retrieved April 3, 2016, from https://www.volkswagenag.com/en/group/strategy.html

Figure

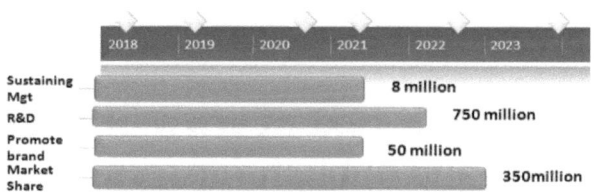

(Volkswagen Group, 2017)